BEI GRIN MACHT SICH IHR WISSEN BEZAHLT

Blockchain Technology Enabled E-Voting System. Challenges, Impacts and Developments

GRIN ☺

Bibliografische Information der Deutschen Nationalbibliothek:

Die Deutsche Nationalbibliothek verzeichnet diese Publikation in der Deutschen Nationalbibliografie; detaillierte bibliografische Daten sind im Internet über http://dnb.d-nb.de abrufbar.

ISBN: 9783346282262
Dieses Buch ist auch als E-Book erhältlich.

© GRIN Publishing GmbH
Nymphenburger Straße 86
80636 München

Druck und Bindung: Books on Demand GmbH, Norderstedt Germany
Gedruckt auf säurefreiem Papier aus verantwortungsvollen Quellen

Das vorliegende Werk wurde sorgfältig erarbeitet. Dennoch übernehmen Autoren und Verlag für die Richtigkeit von Angaben, Hinweisen, Links und Ratschlägen sowie eventuelle Druckfehler keine Haftung.

Das Buch bei GRIN: https://www.grin.com/document/901056

SRH BERLIN UNIVERSITY OF APPLIED SCIENCES

M.SC. COMPUTER SCIENCE FOCUS ON CYBER SECURITY

BLOCKCHAIN AND CRYPTOCURRENCIES

SEMINAR REPORT

Blockchain Technology Enabled E-Voting System

June 11, 2020

Abstract:

Voting is an essential tool for any democratic government, it's the most important factor which makes government for the people and by the people, until now the paper ballot has been used for voting in most countries of the world where voters mark their vote on the paper and put it in the ballot box and at the end of election the votes are counted, but the biggest disadvantage of this system is that it cannot be automated and voters have to physically go to the location for voting that makes the entire process very time consuming and expensive, also digital ballots are vulnerable to hackers and results can be compromised, with the Blockchain technology and cryptography any user can login in GUI using the credentials provided by national election authority and cast their vote by signing it with their private key and trusted miners could verify whether the votes are legit or not by using voter's public keys that makes the entire e-voting process transparent, cost effective, safe and secure.

The proposed system consists of a GUI, an application interface, central database, Blockchain network. Pre-election registration process, voting, counting, final election results and auditing were explained. The consensus algorithm was proof-of-work, all the election properties such as validity, privacy, individuality, flexibility etc. were satisfied.

Contents

List of Figures

List of Tables

1 Introduction

Blockchain technology is a rapidly evolving technology.We remember the times when we used internet just to send e-mails, and none of us ever thought we would use it for online shopping, banking etc.Looking at the current development in Blockchain technology we can surely ensure that we are heading for a next revolution, Blockchain solves the problem of any valuable transfer on the World Wide Web without an intermediary third party, Each block in the Blockchain contains (data, hash, hash of previous block), the data inside the block can differ across multiple scenarios, all the contents of the block are identified using the hash which can differ with any change in the block therefore hash act as a fingerprint, hash of previous block helps in building a Blockchain by acting as a pointer by referring to itself in the next block in Blockchain, and because of the decentralized distributed ledger all the transactions and value associated with it can be verified accurately in the P2P network using the Proof of Work and creating a consensus. [1]

Due to its evolving nature, new economic models can be created and deployed in the Blockchain which are not just limited to financial sector, with the help of self-executing 'Smart Contracts' which are stored on the Blockchain and can be programmed to automate the processes based on various constraints/rules defined in the contract, These contracts can be used across multiple sectors like Storing secure medical records, Trading, Insurance, Electronic voting etc.

In this report we are going to talk about electronic voting systems, requirements, strengths and challenges associated with them.We will explore more on Blockchain technology including benefits, impacts, risks in implementing the Blockchain based electronic voting system, then we will touch upon the current e-voting projects, finally we will describe our proposed model for E-Voting system and conclude this report. [1]

2 E-Voting Systems:

When we talk about E-Voting, we recognize it has been discussed for years in several ways that how to use the electronic technology to make people participate in the election digitally by registering their votes electronically. [2, 3]

Only some countries are already using e-voting systems in elections, India use voter verified paper audit trail (VVPAT) machines for both Municipal and National elections in which voter can verify for whom they voted, and the stored results can be audited multiple times.[4]

Country like Estonia where 99% of public services are now online have been using internet voting i.e. I-voting platform since 2005 for all its elections. [5, 6] Before implementing any system there are security measures, constraints and requirements which are needed to be looked after.

2.1 E-Voting advantages:

- Accurate results and speed in vote count
- Low cost of setup because just internet connection cost is required to vote across all the available e-voting platforms
- Enhanced security as voting take place over secure communication channels
- Accessibility from any corner of the world just by having an internet connection
- Fraud prevention due to less human intervention therefore avoiding the fraud that could possibly take place at the polling stations
- Reduced influence by family members or peers as voters can change their opinion until end of the voting day several times as only the last vote will be considered [4]

Table 1: E-Voting Requirements [1, 3]

Property	Description
Validity	Only the eligible users must be able to vote
Individuality	A voter must not be able to be authorized to vote more than once
Privacy	No one else except voter should know for whom the voter cast the vote
Accuracy	No one must be able to alter, duplicate or destroy the vote
Untraceable	No voter should be able to provide proof of the way he cast his vote
Verifiable	To develop trust in the e-voting system voter should be able to confirm that his vote was received, and the voter should be able to verify that all the votes were counted correctly
Evaluation(Audit)	Election authorities must be able to audit and certify the complete election process by making sure that no illegal means were used
Flexibility	All the eligible voters must be able to cast their vote irrespective of their geographical location
Availability	There must be no down time of the voting systems(Website/ Servers) must function well
Convenience	The voting system should have good usability interface and minimal complexity to complete the voting process so that everyone including the differently abled people could vote without any hassle
Error Detection and Security	Use of secure communication channels and if something fails then data should be recovered until that point

2.2 E-Voting disadvantages:

- In many developing countries internet access is not available to everyone, example: In rural areas low wage workers could not afford internet also many people don't know how to use and access the web

- E-voting machines use software to register the vote and it is built by a company, general public don't know how a software works that might lead to fraudulent results being generated, vendors could also be bribed and in return they could tweak the software to work in their favor

- In the internet voting voter has to login by providing their personal and ID details, which will result in "Voter Anonymity" issue

- There are situations when machine don't produce accurate results due to some errors,malfunctions,along with the possibility of hacking [4, 6]

3 Blockchain technology overview:

In 2008, with the release of bitcoin paper by Satoshi Nakamoto the first concept of Blockchain implementation came into the world and gave rise to a new generation of technology called Blockchain technology that combines cryptography and distributed computing which were already there for decades,and now both of these are combined to create a model where network of computers collaborate to maintain a shared and secure database therefore Blockchain technology is simply a distributed secured database. [7]

The distributed database consists of a string of blocks where each block is a record of data that has been encrypted and provided by a unique identifier called 'hash', then there are miners on the network which validate the transactions and add them to the Blockchain and then the miner broadcast the completed block to the other nodes on the network so that every node has latest copy of the database. [1, 7]

There is no centralized authority which verifies the transaction in Blockchain, it uses the 'Distributed Consensus Algorithm' where all the nodes in Blockchain network must agree about its state so that any single node could not alter the block without consensus of others, once all the nodes arrive at a common consensus the block will be permanently added to the continuously growing list of blocks forming a chain of data blocks.

As shown in the above figure, Series of blocks are chained together and whenever the participants generate any new data the new blocks are formed,each block is represented by the hash value, which is unique for the data within that block.

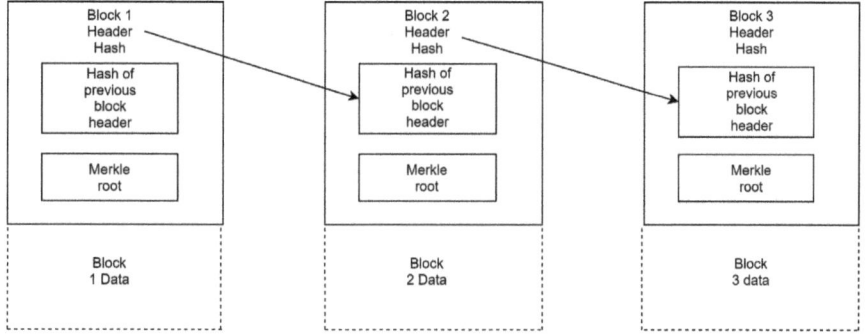

Figure 1: Series of Blockchain

The hashing takes place using a standard algorithm which convert the data in block into 64 characters hash,it can always be recalculated to confirm that the original content have not changed. All blocks formed after the first block are chained with the hash value of the previous blocks meaning, the hash value of the next block is dependent on hash value of previous block therefore the data in any given block cannot be changed without changing all the upcoming blocks after it due to which it's almost impossible to alter data in the Blockchain database once it's written there and cannot be corrupted.

3.1   Network Consensus:

As Blockchain is a distributed system there is no centralized system which can certify the entries of blocks in Blockchain database, the database in maintained by large group of networks called nodes, they are provided with incentive tokens as they use their computing resources to solve mathematical problem.

As not all nodes could be trusted in the large group of P2P networks, so it requires system to provide a mechanism by which all nodes could arrive to a consensus. [1]

Proof of Work:

Mining nodes solve the mathematical problem, verify the transaction, add the transaction to their block and then broadcast the complete state of the block to other nodes on the P2P network.

Every node is required to use its significant resources and try towards solving a complex cryptographic hash function problem, the first node which solves the problem wins the reward for their effort in terms of let's say bitcoin in this case and along with a small transaction fee.

There is no chance of hacking a Blockchain network because of distributed computing mechanism, if some nodes try to manipulate the block then their block will not match with other nodes in the Blockchain thus would not be accepted, if to tamper with the Blockchain all blocks on the network needs to be altered and solve hash algorithm for every block, that requires a control of more than 51% of the P2P network which is not profitable and almost impossible to do. [1]

3.2 Smart Contracts:

Smart contracts are the key innovation of Blockchain 2.0, They consist of a computer code which is stored inside a Blockchain and encoded with contractual agreements. Smart contracts are self-executing which consists of lot of agreements written in terms of lines of code. They remove the need of any third party.

Let's assume a group of ten people would like to make a combined investment to earn interest on their invested funds, then a smart contract could be programmed in such a way which take the interest, then divide it among ten people and send the amount to the wallets of all the stakeholders involved. [1]

Smart contracts just act like a user on the Blockchain that is controlled by the code and not a user, they are immutable and distributed therefore cannot be maliciously changed by any individual or organization also they are verified by all the users on the Blockchain network, hence it can be said that "Code Is Law". [1]

4 Blockchain enabled E-Voting:

In any election there is a central authority which manages and checks all the votes and ensures that the complete voting process is fair but in the Blockchain enabled e-voting the whole process is decentralized, therefore everyone will have a copy of all the voting records with them. The personal data of the voters is encrypted to protect their identities, the biggest advantage is that no authority or groups of people could alter the votes once they are added on the Blockchain because of Blockchain being immutable and distributed also any authorized voter could just vote from anywhere in the world by using the internet instead of queuing up at the polling booth on the voting day. [8, 9]

The Blockchain enabled e-voting system could be implemented from scratch which reflects the characteristics of the electorates or it could also be implemented on a Blockchain system like bitcoin which is already established and is more secure.

Blockchain enabled voting system could also be encoded with smart contracts to automatically generate the results after vote count is done like a self-implementing manifesto. [8, 9]

5 Opportunities and benefits:

The Blockchain based voting system can help to solve many of the problems faced in the recent election process. Each vote has its significant importance and any misuse could result in an unfair election. Blockchain helps to solve many such problems in current voting methods such as ballot and paper voting. [10]

1. **Transparency:** Transparency helps improve voter registration and raises people's trust in the democratic process. Blockchain can help bring more trust at each stage of the voting. It can be used to calculate the votes and storing on the unchangeable public ledger which essentially can be tracked and is visible to everyone. [10]

2. **Accessibility and Affordability:** Blockchain will help to inspire more citizens to vote and take part in the election cycle. People can vote using their mobile anytime and shouldn't have to drive or wait in long lines. Last year, utilizing Blockchain-based technology, people with disabilities voted in the US election.

3. **Security:** Security plays a vital role in securing election results. By using Blockchain, votes could be verified as soon as the voting is over to ensure that they are all correctly counted. By using Blockchain, voting procedures can be made more secure. [10]

4. **Privacy:** During the election, people want privacy while voting, this problem could be solved with the use of Blockchain which enables anonymity. By improving privacy, people will have greater confidence in the system, and vote more likely. [10]

5. **Online Voting:** The voting device is physically placed at different locations and finally the devices are eventually moved to a single

location for counting. [10]

By utilizing Blockchain, we will remove and render it more efficient, all those problems relevant to the present voting mechanism. [10]

6 Challenges, Impacts and Developments:

6.1 Challenges in Blockchain Voting:

The usage of Blockchain in large-scale voting faces several problems. Most citizens have very limited knowledge of the workings Blockchain working. Another very critical problem of electronic elections is that it is impossible to detect potential anomalies. Whereas voting on paper and ballot paper has been studied and investigated for decades. [11]

1. **No Large Scale Testing:** All the experiments are carried out around the world on a small scale, and no large-size analysis was conducted to determine the restriction. In U.S., all small-scale testing was performed where military personnel stationed overseas vote electronically. [11]

    In 2018, the State allowed citizens living abroad to vote using an application called Voatz during a local election in West Virginia. [11]

2. **Challenge other than Blockchain:** There are various problems other than Blockchain related to the functioning of the voting process. The photo ID issued by a government is usually very old and the image used is of poor quality and causes difficulty in facial recognition. [11]

    The facial recognition systems have high error rates, including those used by Voatz even when dealing with current images, especially for non-white voters. [11]

The phone or device used by a voter to cast a ballot might not be secure either –so it is not safe to say that the computer networks they communicate are free from abuse or even accidental errors, and the servers on which the data is stored are protected. [11]

6.2 Impact and Developments:

Blockchain has been recognized by elected officials, entrepreneurs, and even Democratic presidential nominee as a possible way to improve voting and public confidence in election results. [11]

Encouraging signs that Blockchain-based voting could make voting more convenient, thus boosting voter participation. Blockchain technologies can be successful in ensuring computers, networks and vital infrastructure, such as power grids, are protected and personal privacy preserved.[11]

The few small-scale experiments that have been conducted so far have found concerns and flaws in automated networks and government administrative processes that need to be fixed before Blockchain-based voting can be deemed secure and effective.[11]

Companies are now trying to carry the Blockchain to the voter base. One such company is "Horizon State". Participants can use decision tokens (HST) to cast their ballots from a cell phone or Laptop, which are then loaded into an unchangeable database and used to validate the election outcomes securely. Then there is no manipulation, mistake logging, or hacking. However, this system is helpful more than voting, simply for making decisions in an environment where assets and responsibility are shared. [12]

There are several and diverse use cases for the Blockchain voting software. The opportunity to engage and sustain an electoral base is vital for the future of democratic democracy, not just to deliver a straightforward outcome but also to encourage more members to enter the community. [12]

The platform is clearly in its beginning stage, but it is evolving alongside the millennial people whom it can support one day and looking like a vital component of our better tomorrow. [12]

7 Current E-Voting Projects in the Market:

1. Voatz:

Voatz is a decentralized election framework that enables mobile voting by taking advantage of the security found in the latest iterations of smartphone apps and the immutability of the Blockchain. [13]

Key points:

(a) Founded in 2015

(b) The Voatz app is designed with encryption mechanisms installed in compatible smartphones and utilizes Blockchain technologies to guarantee that votes are checked and processed immutably on various, geographically distributed, checking servers until they are sent. [13]

(c) Modern smartphones provide hardware-based security for the storage of private keys that, in turn, enable highly secure, encrypted transactions on the public Internet. [13]

(d) Votes are held on a permitted ledger that would ultimately be managed by different shareholders (such as a Secretary of State or a state election board) to guarantee their resilience and immutability to exploitation. [13]

Case Study: Pilot Project implemented in State of West Virginia,2018

The State of West Virginia used Voatz's electronic voting platform in the first usage of Blockchain technology in a U.S. Federal election to allow foreign citizens to take part in mid-term US elections in 2018. [13, 14]

The pilot attracted a minimum of 144 electors from 31 nations. The application Voatz depends heavily on Blockchain technology to create an unchanging record of the actual votes. [13]

It also uses Cyber security tools to spot viruses on devices and to recognize and authenticate bio-metrics. [13, 14]

2. **Votem:**

Votem is a mobile voting network built on Blockchain that enables people around the world to vote conveniently electronically with unparalleled verifiability, openness, protection and accountability. [15]

Case Study: Rock and Roll Hall of Fame, 2017 and 2018 Inductee Voting, USA:

In 2017, music lovers were able to vote for the 2018 inductee into the Rock and Roll Hall of Fame utilizing Votem's Blockchain-powered smartphone voting app. [15]

Votem processed more than 1,8 million votes without any kind of fraud, compromise, attacks or hacking, marking it with the greatest use of online voting using Blockchain technology to date. Previously the Votem method was used for the Inductee Vote for 2018. [15]

3. **TIVI:**

Smartmatic and Cybernetica established a multidisciplinary research and development Centre in 2014, which aims to advance online voting on a global scale. The outcome of that successful partnership is TIVI. [16]

Study: Utah Republican Party,2016 Presidential Candidate Election, USA

In 2016, Smartmatic-Cybernetica provided the world's first electronic voting utilizing Blockchain technologies to the Utah Republican Party.

Ninety percent of voters enrolled for electronic voting. The platform allowed 24,486 voters to cast their ballots securely using their computer, tablet or smartphone from 45 different countries. [16]

4. Luxoft:

It is a software engineering and digital transformation company offering IT solutions tailored to the needs of customers globally that drive business change. Luxoft's strategy, consulting, and engineering services enable digital business transformation, enhance customer experiences and boost operational efficiency. [17]

Case Study: Switzerland's First Blockchain-Based Vote

More than 220 citizens in Zug have a registered digital ID and were permitted to vote on the app, and approximately 100 replied to the City's survey following the June 25 and July 1 Blockchain-based municipal referendum. [17]

The results show that most people support the possibility of further Blockchain-based e-votes; 79% accept the city's usage of e-voting,with just 2% opposing it.

In fact, 52 percent believe that the advent of e-voting will allow voting quicker and cheaper than filling out a vote. Given the high level of resident support, some remain skeptical about e-voting protection. [17]

Though 21 percent agree that Blockchain technology improves the reliability of online voting, 16 percent has security issues. [17]

8 Proposed E-Voting System:

Table 2: Functions

Central Election Authority	Participating Candidates	Voters	Trusted Miners
Candidates Registration	Pre-Registration	Pre-Registration	Mining
Voters Registration		Voting	
Graphical User Interface			
Application Server			
Miners			
Auditing and Final Result			

GUI Interface: The cross-platform GUI provided by the national authority will enable all the candidates and voters to register with their candidate and voter credentials.

Application Server: Application server will receive requests to register candidates and voters also to authenticate the registered candidates and voters and render the dynamic HTML page content back to the user so that user can interact with the system. It will do so with the help of the web gateway which will be installed on the application server.

Authentication Server Application: The server is hosted as an application on the application server to provide user voter authentication . [18]

8.1 Election Process:

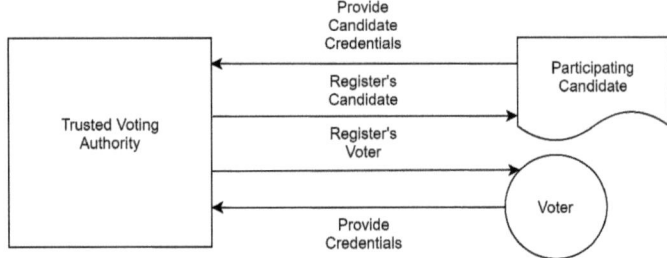

Figure 2: Pre-Election Flow

Pre-Election: Central Election Authority will register candidates, and voters also a trusted network of miners will be established which will be public universities and libraries responsible for broadcasting the approved blocks within the Blockchain network,since Blockchain is a decentralized network central authority could just set various rules regarding size of block, consensus algorithm, auditing of the block and verification of candidates and voters.

Voters will register with their National ID card number and Personal details, then they have to confirm the OTP which will be texted on their registered mobile number after that the voters personal details will get stored in election database and they are matched with National citizens database, if they both match the voters will receive a unique ID and password through which they can login into the election application on the voting day also this received ID and password be encrypted and stored in the election database. [18]

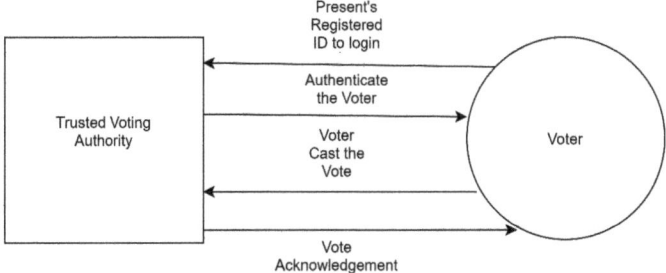

Figure 3: Election Flow

Voting Day:

Voter can login via GUI application using his ID and password provided by the election authority, login details will be passed into the server in encrypted form and will be matched against the stored encrypted details, if they match voter can cast his vote in the next step.

After logging in, voter will receive a digital vote in form of a digital currency, After casting the vote the session will be closed and voter will receive a unique confirmation Id which will be generated from the hash combination of the voter Id, name, voted candidate, and it will have the header value of the prior voter to keep a trace by Election authority,since the unique Id which got generated is in hash,the details cannot be tracked by any other person.

Vote Count: This stage will tell the total vote cast by all the candidates and winner will be declared, trusted miners will add all the consensus block to the Blockchain network, everyone will be able to see who got the most votes, system will auto generate the final results report of overall vote count for every candidate. [18]

19

8.2   Election Network:

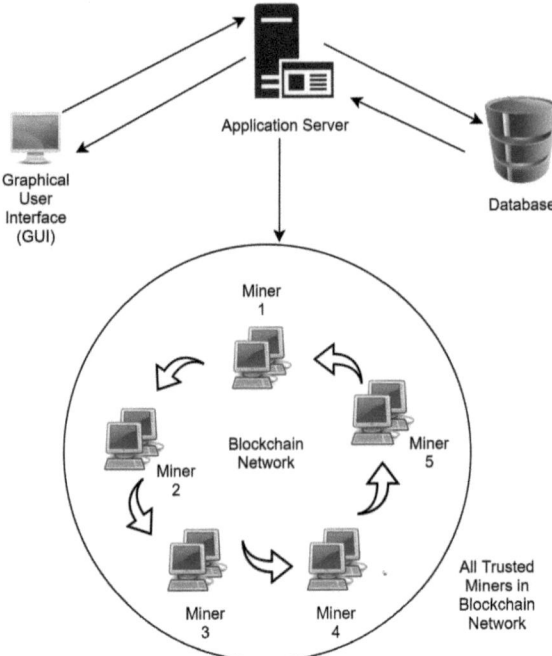

Figure 4: Election System Network Flow

Consensus Algorithm: The proposed system uses the 'proof of work' as its consensus algorithm but since there is negligible computing cost and the miners are all public authorities which are supporting the election process the transaction cost is set to zero and there is no reward for mining the block. [18]

9 Conclusion:

Blockchain technology is relatively a new technology which is constantly evolving year by year with certain new improvements and developments happening in it, although it could take a while for it's organizational and public acceptance.

In this report we have described all the functional requirements, benefits,impacts which are necessary and required for building an e-voting system also we discussed how Blockchain technology can be useful to tackle these issues related to e-voting. We have also touched upon the major current developments of the e-voting projects by popular organizations in form of case study.

Finally, we concluded the report and proposed a basic prototype of an e-voting system based on the Blockchain 1.0 technology which can be later implemented along with the smart contract.

References

[1] J. V. Jorge Lopes, José Luís Pereira. (2019) Blockchain based e-voting system:a proposal. [Online]. Available: https://aisel.aisnet.org/cgi/viewcontent.cgi?article= 1296&context=amcis2019

[2] T. T. S. P. P. V. Robert Krimmer, Henning Tillmann. (2017) Digital democracy: E-voting for everyone? [Online]. Available: https://re-publica.com/en/session/digital-democracy-e-voting-everyone

[3] G. T. Rachid Anane, Richard Freeland. (2018) e-voting requirements and implementation. [Online]. Available: http://www.cs.bham.ac.uk/~rza/pub/evotingReq.pdf

[4] D. T. Peter Wolf, Rushdi Nackerdien. (2011) Introducing electronic voting:essential considerations. [Online]. Available: http://www.corteidh.or.cr/tablas/28047.pdf

[5] [Online]. Available: https://e-estonia.com/solutions/e-governance/i-voting/

[6] [Online]. Available: https://cs.stanford.edu/people/eroberts/cs181/projects/2006-07/electronic-voting/index_files/page0002.html

[7] D. P. Shaun Crawford, Ian Meadows. (2016) Blockchain technology as a platform for digitization. [Online]. Available: https://www.ey.com/Publication/vwLUAssets/EY-blockchain-technology-as-a-platform-for-digitization/$FILE/EY-blockchain-technology-as-a-platform-for-digitization.pdf

[8] P. Boucher. (2016) Scientific foresight unit(stoa). [Online]. Available: https://www.europarl.europa.eu/RegData/etudes/ATAG/2016/581918/EPRS_ATA%282016%29581918_EN.pdf

[9] K. Curran. (2018) E-voting on the blockchain. [Online]. Available: https://www.researchgate.net/publication/329400689_E-Voting_on_the_Blockchain

[10] E. Thompson. (2019) The benefits of blockchain voting. [Online]. Available: https://coinrivet.com/the-benefits-of-blockchain-voting/

[11] N. Kshetri. (2018) Blockchain voting is vulnerable to hackers,software glitches and bad id photos – among other problems. [Online]. Available: https://theconversation.com/blockchain-voting-is-vulnerable-to-hackers-software-glitches-and-bad-id-photos-among-other-problems-122521

[12] J. Liebkind. (2019) How blockchain technology can prevent voter fraud. [Online]. Available: https://www.investopedia.com/news/how-blockchain-technology-can-prevent-voter-fraud/

[13] [Online]. Available: https://voatz.com/faq.html

[14] D. Tambanis. (2019) Blockchain applications: Election voting. [Online]. Available: https://medium.com/bpfoundation/blockchain-applications-election-voting-a1436e7d10cb

[15] [Online]. Available: http://www.votem.com/

[16] (2016) Utah gop caucus voters praise online voting experience. [Online]. Available: https://tivi.io/case/utah/

[17] (2018) Report on switzerland's first blockchain-based vote reveals citizens want more e-voting. [Online]. Available: https://www.luxoft.com/pr/report-on-switzerlands-first-blockchainbased-vote-reveals-citizens-want-more-evoting/

[18] J. S. L. Ishaku Liti Awalu, Park Hung Kook. (2019) Development of a distributed blockchain evoting system. [Online]. Available: https://dl.acm.org/doi/pdf/10.1145/3345035.3345080